AIR FRYER COOKBOOK FOR BEGINNERS

Quick, Healthy, and Delicious Air Fryer Recipes for Beginners with tips and tricks to best use an Air Fryer

Kerry Norris

Table of Contents

TAKE YOUR GIFT

As a way of saying thanks for your purchase,

I'm offering **3 EXTRA BONUSES**:

- ✓ **28-Days Meal Plan**
- ✓ **Shopping List Template**
- ✓ **More Delicious Recipes**

Scan the QR Code with your smartphone and

request your **GIFT now!**

INTRODUCTION

It is no secret that most individuals juggle the need for wholesome, palatable, and quick meals seven days a week. However, the fastest meal options are usually unhealthy, greasy, and salty. As our lives move at noticeably increased rates, many customers struggle to reconcile excellent, quick, and easy meals. A small kitchen equipment called an air fryer mimics the effects of deep-frying meals without using as much excess fat. Food is put inside the air fryer with very little oil instead of completely submerged in oil to cook it. Then, the meal is "fried" just with hot air. The device warms up to a high temperature when switched on, much like an oven. The hot air is moved around the food you are cooking by fans within the oven. Due to the intense heat and the little quantity of oil on the surface of the meal, it cooks rapidly and has a crispy exterior, just like if it had been fried! The digital display on the majority of air fryers will alert you when the device is finished cooking. The fryer's technology removes calories, fat, and the typical amount of oil needed to prepare fried dishes. This procedure prevents cooking oil from getting on their food and arteries.

The most noticeable changes include boosting motor power, expanding the fryer's capacity, and creating accessory packages specifically for cooking methods, including baking, grilling, and frying several items at once. The Maillard effect is a reaction the air fryer may induce by allowing hot air to pass through it. The chemical process known as the Maillard effect is characterized by effects on sugar reduction and amino acid bonding, and it is named after French scientist Louis-Camille Maillard. Most noticeably, this chemical reaction is responsible for the particular taste and aroma that browned food has. The needs of those who are concerned about their lifestyle and health have been taken into account while developing this innovation. The items that are cooked in the air fryer contain up to 80% less fat. That represents a

significant decrease in the amount of fat you ingest each time you consume fatty meals like popcorn, French fries, and many others.

The machine doesn't only generate food; it also creates sweets like cake, cookies, and more. This machine can almost prepare an unlimited variety of things. In addition to the items you would anticipate from a device with the term fryer in the name, the Air Fryer cook's steaks and chops to perfection. All your breakfast essentials and side dishes will be prepared as long as you utilize the uniquely designed separating trays. Despite being less than ten years old, the Air Fryer has already become a mainstay in many households. The fryer may replace many other kitchen equipment in addition to the types of dishes typically cooked by frying since it can make great meals. The Air Fryer is a fantastic appliance for your kitchen since it offers a variety of essential functions. Continue reading this book to benefit from everything the air fryer offers and create delectable dishes for your family to enjoy.

CHAPTER NO: 1
Introduction to Air Fryer

The air fryer is a common kitchen tool for frying meals including pastries, meat, and potato chips. Heat is applied to the air around the item to create a crispy and crunchy exterior. Air-fried foods are marketed as a more nutritious alternative to deep-fried ones due to their lower calorie & fat content. For results that are equivalent to deep-fried foods in terms of flavor and consistency, air-frying needs just 15 ml of oil.

1.1 What distinguishes an oven from an air fryer?

As mentioned earlier, air fryers employ convection heat, similar to a fan oven, but they have a number of features that make them unique. The size is the largest distinction; as air fryers are countertop devices, they have a smaller capacity than traditional ovens. Due to their compact size, powerful heat source, and ventilator, they can cook food much more fast and frequently more evenly than a normal oven. Additionally, many air fryers need no or little preheating time, making them a useful alternative for accelerating the preparation of dinner, particularly for busy families. The biggest benefit of air fryers over conventional fryers may be their ability to prepare a variety of dishes in half the time.

1.2 How are air fryers operated?

An air fryer uses convection heat instead of heated oil, as a deep fat fryer does to cook food. It employs hot air flow to cook the food similarly to a fan oven. The exterior of the food is flavorfully crisped up using the Maillard process. The majority of air fryers come with perforated baskets and trays that allow

hot air to easily flow near food. The fact that air fryers use barely any oil while yet delivering crisp, golden-brown outcomes is one of the reasons they have a reputation for being a healthier alternative to preparing often high-fat foods. Furthermore, some air fryers, such as the Genius series from Tefal, consist of paddles that automatically stir the food while it cooks, ensuring even frying sans the need for manual turning.

1.3 Types of Air fryers

The correct air fryer may depend on its features, size, and material since so many distinct kinds exist. Some air fryer types resemble a regular oven toaster, while others take the appearance of a basket or paddle. Other air fryer kinds may feature racks that store crispers and trays, while other air fryer types have drawers with detachable baskets. While some air fryers just have one function, others include capabilities like baking, grilling, rotisserie, broiling, frying, and toasting. Air fryers' models differ in capacity, size, noise level, heating temperature,pre-heating speed, visibility, and dishwasher compatibility. It helps to be aware of the characteristics of an air fryer, as well as the advantages and disadvantages of each kind, to make it simpler to choose the ideal one for you and the kitchen.

A better diet is made possible by the use of air fryers since they use less oil and lessen extra fat and oil. It may lower caloric intake by 70–80%. Compared to deep oil fryers that employ a high-heat cooking technique and a substantial volume of oil, utilizing an air fryer is considered safer. It decreases the possibility of spilling, splashing, and being exposed to scorching oil since the majority of air fryers can automatically cook the food in an enclosed container. It also encourages weight reduction since it stays away from deep-fried meals, which are often associated with obesity due to their high fat and calorie content. The many models of air fryers that are offered on the market include the following:

- Cylindrical basket air fryer

Drawers with detachable baskets are included in the cylindrical basket air fryer form. A fan sweeps down the hot air that is heated from the top, evenly heating the meal. Air fryers with cylindrical baskets pre-heat faster than other models, usually in less than two minutes. Because cylindrical air fryers are small, the user has more room in the kitchen. Unlike a conventional oven, these air fryers take up less space, so they do not heat the whole kitchen.

Since the cylindrical air fryer is regarded as a little air fryer and can often hold 3 quarts of food or less, it is ideal for usage by one person or small gatherings. It will be necessary to prepare food in batches if you wish to feed bigger groups of four or more people. Due to the design and opaque covers, little to no food is visible inside a cylindrical air fryer. A cylindrical air fryer is substantially noisier than a convection oven when comparing noise levels; it makes around 65 dB, which is comparable to a vacuum cleaner.

- Basket-type air fryer

A basket-shaped air fryer has a compartment inside which food is cooked. Tiny holes in the basket let air in and heat the food components. Thanks to its design, your meal won't have a chance to soak up oil.

- Oven air fryer

Oven air fryers also use the cylindrical basket fryer's heating method. One distinction is that although cylindrical air fryers lack this function, oven air fryers include racks that hold a crisper and baking pan in place. The kitchen oven air fryer performs a variety of culinary tasks silently, including baking, grilling, rotisserie, frying, broiling, and toasting. The glass door of the oven air fryer, which resembles an oven toaster, allows the user to see within. Putting oven air fryer pieces into the dishwasher makes cleaning up a breeze. Comparing the oven air fryer to cylinder and basket air fryers, the oven air fryer takes longer to heat up. When the pre-heating temperature is

achieved, it may heat the whole space. The oven air fryer requires more counter space since it is bigger than the cylindrical basket fryer. Additionally, it signifies that it can accommodate more food; a typical oven can store food of 25 quarts.

- Paddle-type air fryer

  A paddle-style air fryer is ideal if you want to "set it then forget it," staying true to its rotisserie roots. Food may not always be able to be cooked uniformly in air fryers like the cylindrical or basket-type, giving the impression that one side of the dish is undercooked. These varieties need the operator to pull the food from the oven and stir it because of the uneven cooking.

  An air fryer with a paddle design offers the ease of automatically flipping the food over for the user. The inside paddle glides over the basket to distribute the heated air more evenly around the meal. With this kind of air fryer, users may remove the paddle to expand the frying area and fit bigger items. This contemporary air fryer has a greater area and can prepare a variety of foods, including fries, risotto, curries, frozen food, mixed veggies, and many more.

1.4 What sizes are available for the air fryers?

Different sizes and forms of air fryers are available. The ideal air fryer size for the kitchen will be determined by how many people you want to serve. Here are some recommendations:

- For a single individual who often reheats single servings or tiny portions and likes keeping their food crispy, a small air fryer with approximately two quarts would be ideal. Most of the time, one person can use an air fryer that is cylindrical or basket-type. The finest air fryers for highly busy mobile users are paddle-style air fryers.
- 2 people: A couple who wants to prepare fish or poultry with a side of veggies, reheat leftovers, or add a bit extra crispness to their cuisine will benefit from a 3–4-quart air fryer. The air fryers with paddles or cylindrical baskets often hold enough food for two serves.

- 3-5 people: To feed a larger group without having to batch their meals, a share house or a family may need to utilize a 5-7-quart oven air fryer with racks. An oven air fryer with racks is a better option to pick.

1.5 What factors define the ideal air fryer kind?

- Size, cost, controls, materials, and even how simple it is to clean may influence the finest air fryer. A major consideration when selecting an air fryer is size. The number of people it will serve and the amount of counter space you have in your kitchen may determine the best air fryer. A larger kitchen and users with a large number of people to serve may benefit more from an oven air fryer. Despite their price, air fryers provide excellent value for money because of their usefulness and ease. Depending on the brand, a single air fryer may cost anywhere from 45.64€ to 273.90€. Oven air fryers are often more expensive and on the upper end of the range since they are larger than the other varieties. However, certain cylindrical paddle- and basket-shaped ones with many uses, more space, cutting-edge technology, and mobility may also be costly.
- Material for air fryers is crucial to take into account. Cheaper air fryers are composed of plastic with a metal basket, which may harm the environment and your health. When heated, the plastic may release hazardous compounds, including phthalates, that can directly contact food. Teflon or other chemical nonstick coatings may also generate the same outcomes, which may release toxins into the meal. Make sure you choose an air fryer made of stainless steel, coated with ceramics, or made of glass that is PTFE (polytetrafluoroethylene) and PFOA (perfluorooctanoic acid) free. Air fryers typically last two to three years if used 2-4 times a week.
- If used less than twice a week, air fryers may last up to six years. If used daily, cheaper air fryers built of inferior materials may last less than a year. Air fryers might last longer with frequent cleaning. It can be worthwhile for folks who are always moving to check into air fryer models that feature dishwasher-safe components or devices that conveniently fit in a conventional sink. The ability to quickly and easily remove a drawer makes it ideal for cleaning.

- The kitchen's usefulness should be taken into account when choosing the best air fryer. It relates to how kitchen appliances operate and are built, which makes them simpler to use. It is crucial to carefully arrange appliances and other objects in a tiny kitchen to make the most of the available space. Choose an air fryer that will let you use your countertop space to the fullest. Choose one that is sufficiently small if you feel the need to keep it on a shelf while not in use. However, a big oven air fryer with racks and enough room to fit 9" baking pots or 9" casseroles would be ideal if countertop space is not an issue.

1.6 Several strategies for using an air fryer?

An air fryer may be used in several ways. An air fryer may be used for frying, baking, grilling/broiling, roasting/rotisserie, and toasting. An air fryer may give you the extra-crisp, oven-baked flavor of your food that you want without the fat. However, you may be better off using a normal deep oil fryer if you're hoping for a crackly, deep-fried texture with that gooey feeling.

- **Frying:** frying is possible using an air fryer, as the name implies. You can throw wet takeout fries into the air fryer to restore their crispiness. You can cook without using oil if you use an air fryer. The food will have a crunchier texture if you opt to apply oil before air frying (no oil may be applied within the device).

- **Broiling and Grilling:** An air fryer can cook your preferred dinner without needing to continually turn the meat, whether chicken breast or steak. It is simpler to take out and re-insert the grill as necessary since most air fryer models include a grill pan or grill layer with a handle. Your meal will be effectively grilled in an air fryer because it permits hot air to circulate evenly within the appliance and around the food. Because the surface of the grill can quickly absorb any fat or oil residue, it also results in a healthier option.

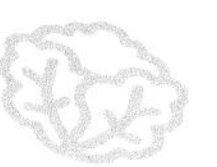

- Baking: Although uncommon, it is possible to bake in an air fryer. You have the option of baking handmade cupcakes, bread, cannoli, donuts, brownies, or even S'mores or heating ready-made pastry products!
- Rotisserie and roasting: For a fast and simple supper, you may use an air fryer to roast veggies and meats. Food cooked in an air fryer is healthier and more quickly than in a conventional oven.
- Toasting: Using an air fryer, you can toast bread. Simply spread olive oil or butter on top of the slice, place it in the air fryer, and set the timer for 2 to 5 minutes at 160° C to produce air fryer toast.

1.7 Benefits of Using an Air fryer

Food that has been air-fried vs deep-fried may be healthier in several ways. Compared to commercially fried foods, they have less fat, calories, and even some potentially harmful ingredients. As you're attempting to lose extra pounds or limit the intake of fat, substituting to an air fryer is a good substitute for deep-frying. The following is a summary of the main advantages of utilizing an air fryer:

- Using an air fryer may reduce the amount of fat.

  Dishes cooked using alternative cooking techniques often contain less fat than foods that have been deep-fried. For instance, a fried chicken breast has more fat than a roasted chicken breast of the same size. According to some companies, frying meals in an air fryer, as opposed to a deep fryer, may reduce the amount of fat in the dish by up to 75%. This is due to the fact that compared to conventional deep fryers, air fryers use substantially less fat for cooking food. Unlike air-fried meals, which only need roughly 15ml of oil, numerous deep-fried food recipes ask for up to 750 ml of oil. As a result, up to 50 times more oil may be needed for deep frying than for air frying.

Despite the fact that the meal doesn't always absorb all of the oil, employing an air fryer may drastically reduce the amount of fat in the final product. According to studies comparing french fries that had been air-fried vs those that had been deep-fried had different qualities at the end, with much less fat and crispy texture but a comparable moisture content and color. This may greatly impact your health. According to several research, consuming more fat from vegetable oils is linked to a greater risk of diseases, including inflammation and heart disease.

Results are contradictory, however, and some evaluations of data imply that dietary lipids from vegetable oil candiminish the risk of heart disease

- The air fryer is safe, fast and easy to use

The air fryer first appeared as a form of deep frying substitute. Even while it was great, it wasn't enough to persuade most people that they needed one since, in any case, not many people regularly use deep fryers at home. We all want to cook more often, but we just do not have the time to do it. Because of this, even though we are aware of how harmful quick meals and takeout are still quite popular. Would you rather order takeout if you could cook things like salmon or pork chops in the air fryer in less than 20 minutes? Because air fryers are quick and simple to use, cooking at home is a far more alluring choice. The air fryer simplifies supper preparation. Simply season a piece of meat, such as a chicken breast (even if it is frozen), place it in the basket, and set the timer for cooking. So easy.

- Crispy and Crunchy Food

You'll enjoy this reason the most if you often prepare frozen and breaded meals like chicken tenders and onion rings. The food you cook in the air fryer becomes crispier as it cooks, giving it a crispy, golden outside instead of a soggy mess. To get a crisp and crunchy surface, you must lightly spray cooking oil over the food's outside. Making anything breaded, as well as any frozen or breaded meal, is best done in this manner.

- It is Very Versatile

The air fryer has several advantages beyond merely being a healthier alternative to traditional deep frying. Almost every meal may be prepared in this appliance, from fried chicken to spaghetti squash to dessert. Frozen grocery store foods like pizza rolls, tater tots, and French fries come out perfectly cooked every time. It's so easy that even little children could accomplish it.

- Faster Than Oven Cooking

An important benefit of an air fryer is that it heats up really rapidly, and the moving air helps the food cook uniformly, brown, and get crispy without much of your input. As a result, you may shorten the time you spend cooking. Aside from the fact that it heats up more rapidly than an oven, an air fryer cook's food more quickly than an oven since it is smaller. While it may take an oven up to 10 minutes to pre-heat, most recipes do not actually need any pre-heating time for an air fryer. This implies that you may simply place your meal in the air fryer's basket, slide it inside, set the timer, and have food ready to eat in 10 to 15 minutes. It is a fantastic tool for fast snacks. It is really simple to switch it on, throw in your favorite food, and cook it to perfection in a matter of minutes, whether for a party or after-school treat. In addition to being able to cook the majority of foods in an air fryer, you can also use one to reheat meals. You may wish to reheat food in an air fryer for a few different reasons.

- Reheating meals this way is fast and simple.
- It prevents food from burning or overcooking.
- It is easy.
- It maintains the food's crispness and fresh flavor.

- Easy to Clean

Is there anybody on the planet that likes to clean up after meals? The truth is that this unpleasant process could take away a lot of the pleasure from a beautiful supper. You'll be happy to know that after usage, a good air fryer is also quite easy to clean. It just needs a routine clean, just like any other pot or pan you've used, if you keep up with cleaning it each time you cook in it. Simply use a non-scratch sponge to clean the inside and outside of the basket after filling it with soapy water. Some air fryer baskets may be cleaned in the dishwasher. Depending on how often you use it, you should also give the whole appliance, including the frying coil, a thorough cleaning once or twice a month. In contrast to cleaning the oven, it is not a difficult or time-consuming chore if you do it often.

- Changing to an air fryer might help you lose weight.

Chips fried in an air fryer absorb substantially less oil and have fewer calories when compared to chips cooked in a deep-fat fryer on an equivalent basis. Therefore, by drastically reducing the amount of fat you consume, switching to air frying from deep frying would surely enhance the nutritional value of your diet. However, the majority of air fryers still need oil to be added to meals, that isn't necessarily the healthiest method of cooking food. For instance, air-fried broccoli contains more calories than steamed broccoli, which is cooked without the use of oil. Air-fried foods have to be included in a healthy diet.

Deep-fried foods include more calories and more fat than normal foods, which might result in an increase in weight. A larger intake of fried foods was connected to a higher risk of obesity, according to a significant study review.

If you're attempting to reduce weight, switching to air-fried foods from deep-fried ones can be a beneficial place to begin. With 9 calories for each gram, dietary fat has more than two times as many calories of each gram than other macronutrients & micronutrients like carbs to protein.

Moving to an air fryer is a simple option to consume less calories and help with weight control since air-fried foods have less fat than foods that are deep fried.

- **Using air fryers may reduce the production of dangerous substances**

Fried food has extra fat, calories, and possibly dangerous substances like acrylamide. During meals with a high carbohydrate content are cooked at high heat, such as when frying, the chemical acrylamide is created. The International Agency for Research on Cancer has designated acrylamide as a "probable human carcinogen," which means that some evidence suggests that acrylamide may be related to the development of cancer. The Environmental Protection Agency also determines acrylamide to be "likely to be carcinogenic to humans." Your food's acrylamide concentration may be reduced if you air-fried it rather than deep fry it. Compared to conventional deep-frying, earlier research indicated that air-frying significantly decreased the amount of acrylamide by up to 90%. It is crucial to remember that additional dangerous substances might still be created during the air-frying process. Other potentially hazardous substances produced by high-heat cooking, such as heterocyclic amines, aldehydes, and polycyclic aromatic hydrocarbons, may raise the risk of cancer.

1.8 Tips and Tricks to best use the Air fryer

1. **Before adding your meal, preheat your air fryer.**

Consider your air fryer to be a little oven. If yours doesn't offer a preheat option, let it three to five minutes to warm up before you start cooking. An air fryer advantages from a few minutes of preheating, much like an oven. Simply turn it on before placing your food in the basket to do. It is a straightforward step that many people skip, but it may help you save your cooking time by a few minutes.

2. Be careful to oil the basket of your air fryer, so nothing sticks.

   Although the nonstick coating that most air fryer baskets feature, you should still oil the basket to avoid food sticking. Given that air fryers' internal temperatures may rise to very high levels, oils with high smoking points (such as safflower or soybean oil) are the best for use. Use ordinary (or light-tasting) types of olive oil, which have smoke points between 2148° C and 2593° C, rather than extra-virgin varieties, which have smoky points between 1927° C and 2260° C, if you wish to use olive oil in an air fryer.

   However, avoid using nonstick aerosol cooking sprays, which may harm your air fryer. You should avoid using sprays since they include ingredients that "damage the nonstick coatings of certain air fryer baskets" A simple substitute is buying a spray container and filling it with your own oil.

3. For crispier, tastier leftovers, air fried the meal instead of reheating it in the microwave.

   You can reheat everything from leftover pizza and vegetables to roast chicken and fish in the air fryer. Simply set the air fryer to a lower-than-normal temperature, such as 175° C, to heat your food without overcooking it. The leftovers will be crispy and hot, never mushy or tasteless, after approximately a minute.

4. To avoid smoking, add water to the air fryer drawer before frying fatty meals (such as bacon or chicken thighs).

   Your air fryer may start smoking if you cook foods that release a lot of fat, such as meatballs, bacon, or hamburgers since the fat builds up in the air fryer pan and becomes hot. If this occurs, you may add water to the cooking tray before you begin to prevent it from occurring, or you can stop the machine, drain the fat, and start cooking again. The water will stop the grease from smoking and becoming too hot, and prepare pan sauces and gravies using the drippings that accumulate in the drawer (like bacon grease!).

Even if it has a little water, the fat in that pan is completely usable and flavorful. Do not let it go to waste since you may save it in a Tupperware or jar for later use and use it to make pan sauces, gravies, and other dishes!

5. While cooking, shake the basket a couple of times to ensure everything is cooking equally.

   Give the basket a couple of shakes during cooking to ensure that your goods are cooked evenly. You can simply remove the basket from the air fryer while it is still operating without any issues. This is particularly helpful for small foods like fries or tiny roasted vegetables that you want to crisp all over. It should just take a few shakes to verify that everything is crisp and even.

6. To get the crispiest food, use olive oil moderately rather than liberally.

   Less oil is really better when it comes to air frying since you may believe that covering your meal in gobs of oil would make it crispier. If you use too much olive oil, your dish may get mushy rather than crisp. Use less to get the most taste and texture from your olive oil.

7. Watch out for overcrowding the air fryer basket.

   The air won't be able to flow correctly in your air fryer basket if you put too many objects in it, which will prevent your food from being crispy. Cook ingredients in batches instead of all at once when creating a huge quantity of anything. This guidance is particularly crucial for fries, chopped vegetables, and other little products that you want to make really crispy.

8. Cook bigger foods in one even layer rather than stacking them, such as whole pork chops or chicken cutlets.

   In the air fryer, foods, including steaks, fish fillets, pork chops, and hamburgers, must be fried in a single layer. When you attempt to stack them, the sides that contact one another will become colorless and drenched in moisture. If your air fryer basket can only hold three steaks at once and you want to cook more, you have to cook them in batches.

9. Cleanup will be simpler if you use foil or parchment paper.

To simplify cleaning, you may lay messy foods (like wings covered in a sticky sauce) on a piece of parchment paper or tinfoil put on top of the air fryer basket. Just make that the food is substantial enough to hold it down since the power of the hot air moving might cause the sheets to fly about.

10. Ensure that your air fryer has at least 5 inches of clearance all around it.

Food in air fryers is crisped by hot air circulation; thus, providing adequate room around the appliance on all sides is crucial to allow for optimal air flow. As a general guideline, allow 5 inches of room on all sides and ensure all surfaces are heat-resistant. Pushing an air fryer up against a wall is not a good idea.

11. To avoid spices splattering on your cuisine, combine them with oil before adding them.

Lightweight spices often blow off food in an air fryer because of the powerful air circulation. Mixing the spices with oil and then coating your products in that combination is one approach to prevent this. They are weighed down and adhered to the meal by the oil.

12. Do not confine your tastes to the savory. In an air fryer, "baking" is feasible and quite useful.

Even if your air fryer doesn't have a dedicated baking pan, you can still bake a variety of different foods using a regular oven-safe pan. The sweets you can "bake" in an air fryer are ideal examples, including cakes, brownies, and doughnuts. Consider your device to be a powerful convection oven. Keep an eye on your baked items to prevent them from browning too rapidly since the fan is stronger than a conventional one. If they do, just wrap them in foil and keep "baking" them.

13. Have Fun and Experiment

This advice, in our opinion, is crucial! Enjoy using your air fryer after you've gotten the hang of it. Experiment and expand your horizons! Use your expertise to develop new recipes as you get used to cooking times, breading techniques, and other factors.

1.9 How to use the recipes for 1500 days?

Congratulations, and welcome to the air frying community. For practically all households, counter space in the kitchens is a valuable asset. You may think your kitchen has plenty of counter space, but you'd be shocked at how simple it is to stock it with contemporary cooking tools. Having said that, one of the newest culinary machines you want to make a place for is an air fryer. Ovens, which can roast and even bake your favorite dishes, are readily accessible in practically any shop nearby and perform the same purpose as air fryers. With an air fryer in your kitchen, you can quickly prepare very crisp dishes while using less oil than deep frying. An air fryer often warms up quite rapidly, and the strong heat source and fan help your food cook quickly and evenly.

In contrast to deep frying, air frying does not entail drowning food in oil, making your recipes eatable for many days. In an air fryer, hot air is circulated quickly over food to cook it and create a crispy outer layer via browning processes. Additionally, very little to no cooking oil is utilized during air frying. It follows that you may create people's favorite crispy and crunchy delicacies in an air fryer without using a lot of oil. This cookbook is for you if you like eating healthy fried cuisine. It includes a good number of delectable dishes you may make in the convenience of your own home and can use for 1500 days repeatedly. The components for the recipes in this cookbook are simple to get at your neighborhood supermarket or grocery shop. So you do not need to worry about finding a certain component. However, if you have trouble locating a certain item, feel free to use a comparable one to attain the same effects. Almost all food categories are included in the dishes in this cookbook, including grains, meat, eggs, fish, cereals, fruits, poultry, and vegetables for you to enjoy. Every dish you'll discover in this book is simple

to prepare at home and to enjoy for many days. The recipes are simple to follow, and some of them may even be made by children without an adult's assistance.

Now that you understand the theory behind air frying, are you prepared to start cooking? Every meal of the day may be inspired by the recipes, which also include appetizer and dessert options. Even simply imagining it makes us hungry! Guys, let's do this.

Air Fryer Breakfast Recipes

These simple air fryer breakfast ideas will be your go-to meals on hectic mornings! I've got you covered whether you want a sweet or savory breakfast. The best way to start the day is with one of these air fryer breakfast dishes!

Each dish includes the prep time, cook time, portions, ingredients needed, directions, nutritional inform ation, and sometimes cooking hints if you want to change an item or two or just become better at cooki ng.

1. BREAKFAST BOMBS

All your favorite breakfast ingredients, including crispy bacon, scrambled eggs, and cheese, are combined in these easy to prepare biscuit bombs.

Ingredients:	
14g	of butter
1 tube of refrigerated biscuit dough	
30ml	of whole milk
4	eggs
3g	of finely chopped chives
4 slices of cooked and crumbled bacon	
28g	of melted butter
9g	of poppy seeds (or everything seasoning)
13.8g	of coarse salt

Instructions

1. Add butter to a pan & melt over medium flame. Eggs & milk should be whisked together in a big bowl. In a pan, pour the egg mixture, and let it somewhat set. As soft curds begin to form, lower the heat to medium-low and stir periodically. Add salt &pepper to taste. Add chives after taking the pan off the heat.
2. Form each biscuit into a circle that is 1/4" thick. Add cheese, bacon, and scrambled eggs to the top of each dough round. The dough's edges should be brought together and sealed with a pinch.
3. Spread melted butter over the tops, then season with salt and pepper.
4. Place a piece of parchment paper coated with a cooking spray inside the air fryer's basket, then add biscuit bombs in batches, ensuring sure they do not touch. For ten minutes, or until the biscuits are baked & at 190° C.

Nutritional Info:

Calories 305 kcal, **Carbs** 26g, **Protein** 19g, **Fat** 15g

2. AIR FRYER FRENCH TOAST STICKS

With these simple air fryer French toast sticks, breakfast doesn't have to be skipped. No worry about the skillet being too hot or soaking the ingredients overnight. For stronger, more easily dipped French toast, go for thick-sliced bread.

Ingredients	
80g	of heavy cream
2 large	eggs
79ml	of pure vanilla extract
2.5ml	of pure vanilla extract
0.7g	of ground cinnamon
Maple	syrup for serving
37g	of granulated sugar
6 slices	of white loaf, every slice cut into thirds
Kosher salt	to taste

Instructions

1. In a large shallow baking dish, whisk the eggs, cream, sugar, cinnamon, a dash of salt, milk & vanilla. Bread should be added and given a couple of coats.
2. French toast should be placed in the air fryer's basket in batches as needed to avoid overcrowding. Air fried at 190 degrees Fahrenheit for 8 minutes total, turning once.
3. Drizzle heated bread with maple syrup before serving.

Nutritional Info:

Calories 366 kcal, **Carbs** 48.5g,

Protein 22g,

3. CRISPY AIR FRIED BACON

Ingredients	
340g	of thick-cut bacon

Instructions

1. Place the bacon in one even layer into the air fryer basket.
2. Heat the air fryer to 200° C and cook the food for 10 minutes or until it is crispy. (You may check at the halfway point and use tongs to rearrange pieces.)

Nutritional Info:

Calories 38 kcal, **Carbs** 10g, **Protein** 36g, **Fat** 3.5g

4. AIR FRYER HASH BROWNS

Ingredients	
60ml	of water
140g	of peeled and grated potatoes, preferably russet
3g	of salt
15ml	of vegetable oil

Nutritional Info:

Calories 120 kcal, **Carbs** 15g, **Protein** 1g, **Fat** 6g

Instructions

1. Toss potatoes and water in a medium basin until the potatoes are well coated. Wrap in plastic wrap and make several fork slits in the plastic.
2. Transfer to the microwave and heat, stopping to stir the mixture every minute, for 3 1/2 to 4 minutes, or until the potatoes are nearly completely cooked but still have some bite.
3. Allow the potatoes to cool and after the potatoes have cooled, mix them with salt and oil. When the hash to be handled, shape them into 6 1" thick, rectangular pucks with rounded edges.
4. Heat the air fryer to 200° and air fry the hash browns for 15-20 minutes until they are crispy and golden brown.

5. AIR FRYER DONUTS

Ingredients	
7g	of instant yeast or active dry yeast
250ml	of lukewarm milk
1	egg
360g	of all-purpose flour
50g	of granulated sugar, plus 5g
3g	of salt
	Coconut Oil Spray
57g	of melted butter

Instructions

1. Mix lukewarm milk, 5g of sugar, and yeast in the bowl of a mixer equipped with a dough hook. 10 minutes should pass for it to get foamy.
2. If the milk is too hot or yeast is cold, nothing will happen you have to start over.
3. Add 250g of flour, sugar, egg, salt, and melted butter to the milk mixture. Whisk on low speed until incorporated, then, gradually add the last cup of flour while the mixer is running until the dough is not sticking to the bowl. The dough should be elastic and smooth after 5 minutes of kneading at a medium-low pace.
4. Put the dough in a basin that has been buttered, and then wrap it in plastic. Allow doubling in a warm location. If you press your finger into the dough and the indentation stays, the dough is ready.

8. Butter should be melted in a small saucepan set on medium flame while the donuts are in the Air Fryer. Vanilla essence and powdered sugar should be well combined. When the icing is slightly thin but not runny, remove it from the heat and mix in 15ml of hot water at a time. Place aside.

9. Forks are used to dip hot doughnuts and donut holes into the glaze. Put them on a wire rack on a baking sheet with a rim to catch any extra glaze that may drop off. Allow it to settle for 10 minutes or until the glazing becomes firm.

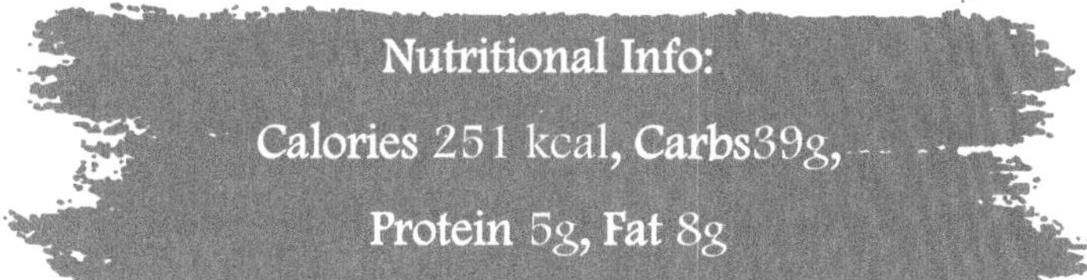

5. The dough should next be rolled out to a thickness of about 1/2 inch on a floured surface. 10–12 donuts may be cut using a circular cutter of 3–12 inches in diameter.

6. Place doughnuts and donut holes on parchment paper that has been gently dusted with flour, then, cover loosely with oiled plastic wrap. Allow doughnuts to rise for 30 minutes or until their volume has doubled. Turn the Air Fryer on at 180 degrees.

7. Donuts should be gently transferred in one even layer to the Air Fryer basket after being sprayed with oil spray. Donuts should be sprayed with oil and cooked for approximately 4 minutes at 180C until they turn golden brown. Continue with the remaining holes and donuts.

6. AIR FRYER CRISPY POTATOES

Ingredients

Ingredients	
15ml	extra-virgin olive oil
450g	of baby potatoes, halved
4g	of garlic powder
5g	of Cajun seasoning (optional)
	Kosher salt and black pepper, to taste
5g	of Italian seasoning
	Lemon wedge for serving
	Freshly chopped parsley, for garnish

Instructions

1. Add oil, Italian seasoning, garlic powder, and Cajun spice with the potatoes in a large bowl. Add salt and pepper to your desired taste.
2. Put the potatoes in the basket of your air fryer and air fry for 10 minutes at 200 C. Shake the basket as you toss and cook the potatoes for a further 8 to 10 minutes, or until they are golden and soft.
3. Before serving, squeeze lemon juice over the boiled potatoes and top with fresh parsley.

Nutritional Info:

Calories 100 kcal, **Carbs** 22g, **Protein** 3g,

7. AIR FRYER CRAB CAKES

Ingredients + For crab cakes	
57g	of mayonnaise
A large egg	
6g	of minced chives
2g	of Old Bay seasoning
10g	of Dijon mustard
15ml	of olive oil cooking spray
2g	of finely grated lemon zest
200 g	of jumbo lump crab meat, cleaned
12g	of kosher salt
120g	of Saltine cracker crumbs (from about 20 crackers)

Instructions

1. To make the crab cakes, combine the egg, chives, mayonnaise, mustard, lemon zest, Old Bay, and salt in a large bowl. Cracker crumbs and Crab meat should be mixed before adding.
2. Make 8 patties from the crab mixture (you can refrigerate the patties for up to 4 hours).
3. Coat the tops of the crab cakes cooking spray. Generously oil spray the air fryer basket as well. Place crab cakes in a basket single layer. Cook for 12 to 14 minutes at 190° C, turning halfway through, until crisp deep golden brown.

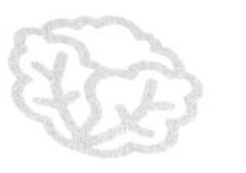

FOR TARTAR SAUCE	
57g	of mayonnaise
5ml	of fresh lemon juice
4g	of finely chopped dill pickle
2g	of finely chopped capers
1g	of chopped fresh dill
Lemon wedges and Hot sauce for serving	
6g	of finely chopped shallot
10g	of Dijon mustard

4. To make the tartar sauce, combine the mayo, pickles, shallot, capers, lemon juice, dill, and mustard in a medium bowl.
5. Serve heated crab cakes with tartar sauce, hot sauce, and lemon wedges.

Nutritional Info:

Calories 387 kcal, **Carbs** 15g,

Protein 24g, **Fat** 25g

8. BACON-WRAPPED AVOCADO

Ingredients	
24	thin strips of bacon
3	avocados
60g	of ranch dressing for serving

Instructions

1. Cut each avocado into 8 wedges of the same size. If necessary, cut a piece of bacon to fit around each wedge.
2. Arrange in an air fryer basket in one even layer while air frying in batches. Cook bacon until fully cooked and crispy for 8 minutes at 200°C.
3. Serve with warm ranch dressing.

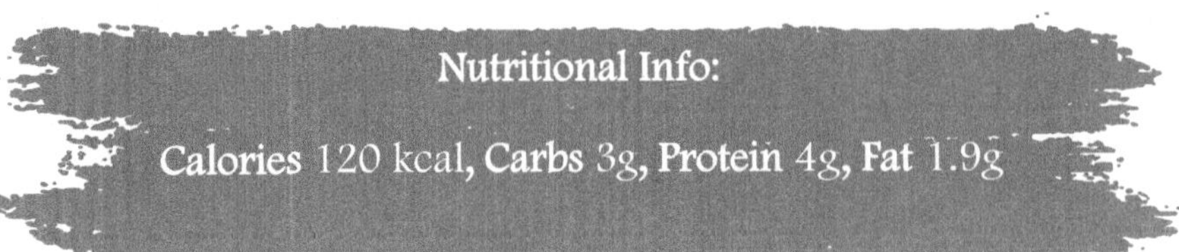

9. AIR FRYER ROASTED VEGGIES

Ingredients	
90g	of diced asparagus
102g	of diced summer squash
112g	of diced zucchini
53g	of diced cauliflower
75g	of diced sweet red pepper
1.4g	of seasoning, or more to taste
10ml	of vegetable oil
50g	of diced mushrooms
0.5g	of black pepper
1g	of salt

Instructions

1. Preheat your air fryer to 180° C.
2. A big bowl should be seasoned with oil, pepper, salt, squash, zucchini, mushrooms, asparagus, cauliflower, and your desired seasoning. Place in the frying basket in one even layer after tossing to coat.
3. Cook in the preheated air fryer for ten minutes, stirring once after half time, until tender-crisp.

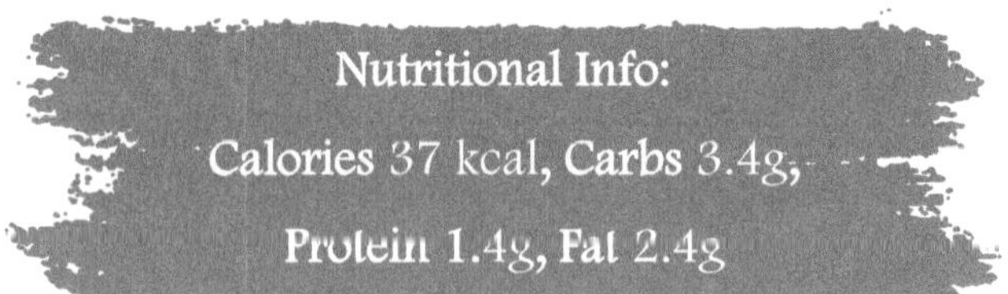

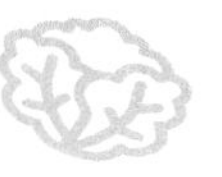

10. AIR FRYER BAKED POTATOES

Ingredients	
2.5g	of sea salt
4	russet potatoes
15ml	of olive oil

Instructions

1. Thoroughly dry potatoes with a towel after washing them under running water.
2. Use a fork to prick the potato, then massage it with oil and salt. Potatoes should be added to the basket of your air fryer.
3. Air Fry the potatoes for 30 minutes at 200°C in a basket-style air fryer. Depending on size, boil the potatoes for a further 5–15 minutes on the other side or until a fork can be inserted all the way easily into the middle. Larger potatoes could take longer to cook than smaller ones. Transfer potatoes to plate using tongs and serve.

Calories 199 kcal, **Carbs** 38g, **Protein** 5g, **Fat** 4g

11. AIR FRYER STRAWBERRY TURNOVERS

Ingredients	
1 567g	can of strawberry pie filling
1	can of Crescent Dough Sheets
10ml	of Water
1	large egg, beaten

Instructions

1. With a fork, seal the edges of the rectangle's other end by folding it over the filling. Make a few piercing on the front of every turnover with the fork.
2. Apply egg wash to the turnovers' tops.
3. Spray the turnovers with oil or coat the air fryer basket with parchment paper, and then place the turnovers inside to cook.
4. Preheat the air fryer to 160C, any leftover turnovers that cannot be cooked at the same time needs to be placed on parchment paper lined baking sheet, till you bake them. Keep them chilled.
5. Bake for 17 minutes.
6. Turnovers that have baked should be taken out of the fryer and placed on a cooling rack. If you can't fit them all in the fryer, continue with another batch of baking.
7. Serve
8. The egg and water should be softly beaten in a small bowl before being placed aside.
9. The thawed puff pastry sheet(s) should be unrolled and cut into eight rectangles.
10. Each rectangle should have about 7g of filling on one end.
11. Around the filling, egg wash the pastry's three

Nutritional Info:

Calories 514 kcal, **Carbs** 66g, **Protein** 5g, **Fat** 4.5g

12. CHOCOLATE CHIP COOKIES

Ingredients	
170g	of softened unsalted butter
250g	of all-purpose flour
67g	of brown sugar
4g	of vanilla
200 g	of sugar
2	large eggs
2g	of salt
340g	of chocolate chips
2.8g	of baking soda

Nutritional Info:

Calories 516 kcal, **Carbs** 68g, **Protein** 6g, **Fat** 4.8g

Instructions

1. Add the butter, white, and brown sugar in a large bowl& mix well. The butter and sugars should be well blended and creamy.
2. Salt, baking soda, vanilla, eggs, and half of the flour should be added. Mix the dry ingredients with the butter mixture until well-mixed.
3. When the cookie dough is thick and creamy, add the remaining half of the flour & beat on medium speed until combined. After the dough has been combined, whisk in the optional nuts and chocolate chips to distribute them evenly.
4. The dough should be molded using a tiny cookie scoop or spoon. On top of the parchment paper, put the dough balls in the air fryer basket. Each cookie should have an inch or so between them.
5. For 7-8 minutes, air fry at 150 degrees Celcius Before moving the golden-brown cookies to the cooking rack, let them rest in the basket of the air fryer for an extra one to two minutes.

13. AIR FRYER GRILLED SHRIMP

These juicy, plump, and well-seasoned air-fryer grilled shrimp are delicious! This nutritious breakfast may be made in only 8 minutes using ingredients in most kitchen cabinets.

Ingredients	
450g	of shrimp
1g	of garlic powder
0.5g	of paprika
1g	of Italian seasoning
10ml	of olive oil
1g	of black pepper
3g	of salt

Ingredients

1. Remove the shrimp's veins and shells to clean them. Run under running water, then, blot with paper towels to dry.
2. In a small bowl, mix the seasoning and oil.
3. Using the seasoning mixture, coat the shrimp on both sides and let them sit for 15 minutes.
4. Use the skewers after dipping them in water for 15 minutes. This will stop the skewers from browning while we are grilling. The shrimp are now skewered in and kept ready.
5. Put shrimp in one even layer in the basket or rack of an air fryer.
6. Cook for 8 minutes at 200° C.
7. Serve.

Nutritional Info:

Calories 134 kcal, **Carbs** 1g, **Protein** 23g, **Fat** 4g

CHAPTER NO: 3

Air Fryer Lunch Recipes

Here are some healthy recipes to get you started on your cooking. These dishes made in an air fryer are crispy, rich, and delectable. To show just how flexible an air fryer can be, check out this comprehensive list of our favorite air fryer recipes. If you do not already own one, use this as a cue to get one.

1. AIR FRYER FRENCH FRIES

Ingredients

15ml	of extra-virgin olive oil for drizzling
Sea salt to taste	
2	russet potatoes, cut into ¼" of sticks
Chili powder, herbs, or chipotle powder	

Dips and optional seasonings:

Mayo, ketchup, chipotle sauce or mustard

Instructions

1. Set the air fryer's temperature to 193° C and preheat.
2. Add salt and olive oil to the potatoes before tossing them to coat.
3. Arrange the potatoes in your air fryer basket in one even layer without letting any of them come into contact. Work will have to be done in groups. Until crispy, cook for 12 to 15 minutes, turning halfway through. Air fry your fries for a little while longer if they aren't crispy.
4. After all the batches have been completed, place them in air fryer for reheating (there is no need to arrange them in one even layer) for 1–2 minutes to reheat and re-heat any that were cold during the initial batches.
5. Serve with the desired dips & spices.

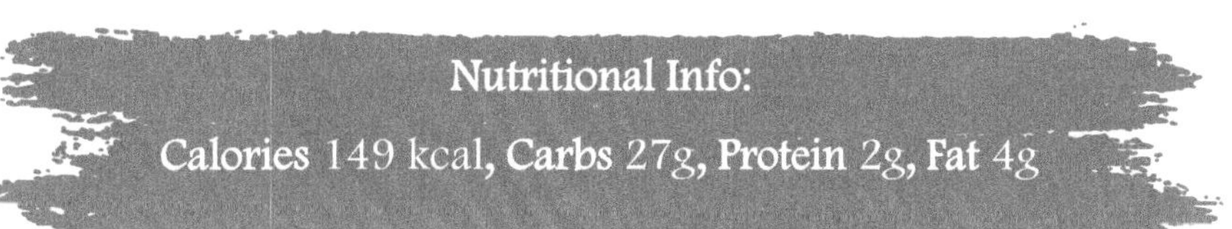

2. AIR FRYER ONION RINGS

Ingredients	
1g	of paprika
6g	of salt, divided t
1	egg
63g	of all-purpose flour
118ml	of buttermilk
1	large sweet yellow onion, cut into half-inch thick
7ml	of olive oil
60g	of panko breadcrumbs
of panko breadcrumbs	

Nutritional Info:

Calories 193 kcal, **Carbs** 26g, **Protein** 5g, **Fat** 4.5g

Instructions

1. 4 deep plates are required for this recipe. Mix paprika, flour, and 3g salt in the first dish. Add the buttermilk (or milk and lemon/vinegar juice), egg, and the flour mixture (30g) in the second dish. Add the panko breadcrumbs, olive oil and 3g teaspoon salt in the third dish, mix well with a fork. Place half of the panko in a fourth bowl and use it to switch to the second part after the first got sticky.
2. To remove excess moisture, pat the onion rings with paper towels. The onion rings should be dredged with a fork in the flour mixture, placed in the buttermilk mixture, and then coat in the panko mixture. (TIP: Freeze your breaded onion rings on a sheet for approximately 15 minutes to help the panko mixture adhere better.)
3. Oil spray the air fryer basket generously. Add the onion rings in one even layer in the Air Fryer basket. You can place small breaded onion rings inside the big ones, keep some space in between them there should be no touching.
4. Air fry for 11 to 15 minutes at 200° C or until they turn golden brown and crunchy. After around 6 minutes, apply some cooking spray. The onion rings do not need turning.
5. With a cookie spatula or fork, carefully remove the onion rings and serve.

3. AIR FRYER CHICKEN WINGS

Ingredients	
900g	of chicken wings without tips & split at joints
15ml	nonstick cooking spray
125ml	of Frank's Red Hot sauce,
56g	of butter
Blue or Ranch cheese dressing for serving	
Kosher salt to taste	

Instructions

1. Cooking spray has to be applied to a 3.5-quart air fryer basket. With paper towels, pat the chicken wings dry before salting them. Do not let the wings contact when you place them in the fryer basket. After cooking the wings for 12 minutes at 182 degrees Celsius, turn them over using tongs and continue cooking for another 12 minutes. The wings should cook for 6 minutes after being turned over, with the heat increasing to 200 degrees C.
2. Meanwhile, microwave the butter in microwave for approximately 60 seconds or until melted. Add in the spicy sauce by whisking.
3. In a big bowl, coat the wings with the butter mixture and serve with the dressing.

Nutritional Info:

Calories 302 kcal, **Carbs** 6.5g, **Protein** 29g, **Fat** 17.

4. AIR FRYER POTATO AND BROCCOLI

Ingredients	
250ml	of reduced-fat milk divided
4 medium russet potatoes (174g to 198g. each)	
16g	of all-purpose flour
6g	of kosher salt
117g	of extra-sharp shredded Cheddar cheese, divided
90g	of chopped broccoli florets
Chopped chives for garnishing	
0.5g	of cayenne pepper

Nutritional Info:
Calories 129 kcal, **Carbs** 23g, **Protein** 6g, **Fat** 2g

Instructions

1. Use a fork to pierce potatoes all over. Place on a microwave-safe dish and heat for 5 minutes on high, five more minutes in the microwave after turning the potatoes.
2. In the meanwhile, boil 177ml of milk to a simmer in a pan on a medium-high flame. The remaining milk and the flour should be combined with a whisk in a small bowl. Mix the flour mixture until smooth before adding it to the pan. While continuously whisking, let it come to a boil. Get rid of the heat. Save about 30g of the cheddar. Once smooth and mixed, stir in the remaining Cheddar. Salt, cayenne, and broccoli into a bowl.
3. The potatoes should be cut in half; then, the insides should be gently mashed until they are crumbly and loose. Four potato halves should be placed in the basket of an air fryer at once. 15g of Cheddar is then scattered among the potatoes after topping each with 18g of your broccoli mixture.
4. About 5 minutes into cooking the potatoes at about 180 degrees C, the potato skins should be crisp and cheddar should be melted. Repeat with the remaining Cheddar, potatoes, and broccoli combination.
5. If preferred, garnish the potatoes with chives before serving.

5. AIR FRYER TWICE BAKED POTATOES

Ingredients	
30g	of sour cream
117g	of cheddar cheese
2 cooked, baked potatoes	
2 slices of bacon, cooked	
14g	of butter

Instructions

1. Scoop the insides of the cooked potatoes into a bowl after cutting them in half.
2. Add the sour cream, butter & 58g of cheddar cheese to the bowl of potatoes.
3. Use a potato masher to combine the ingredients and mash the potatoes until they are the appropriate consistency.
4. Re-spoon the ingredients into the potato shells, piling them up.
5. Keep chilled until you're ready to serve.
6. The potatoes should be placed in an air fryer basket at the time of baking. Air fry for 8 minutes at 200° C.
7. Bacon pieces and the rest of the 59g of cheddar cheese are sprinkled on the potatoes. As doing this, make sure to keep your hands save from hot surface of the air fryer.
8. To crisp the bacon& for cheese melting, potatoes back in the air fryer and air fry for about 3 minutes more at 200° C.

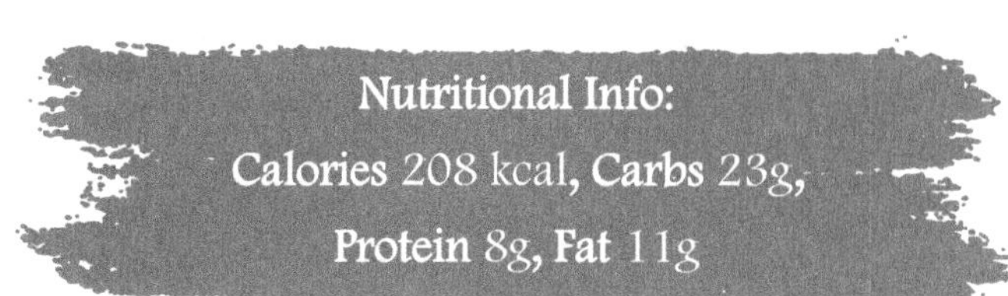

6. BUFFALO BITES

Ingredients	
30ml	of olive oil
43g	of melted butter
45g	Buffalo wing sauce
1 small head cauliflower, broken into florets	
Dip	
32g	of plain Greek yogurt, fat-free
56g	of crumbled blue cheese
Celery sticks, optional	
350g	of cottage cheese
1 packet of ranch salad dressing mix	

Instructions

1. Preheat the air fryer to 180 degrees. Cauliflower and oil are combined in a big basin and mixed to coat. Cauliflower should be placed in the air fryer basket in single layers in batches.
2. Air fry for 10 to 15 minutes, stirring halfway through or until the edges are browned, and the florets are soft.
3. Melted butter and Buffalo sauce should be mixed in a big basin. Add the Cauliflower and coat it. Transfer it to the serving dish. Mix the ingredients for the dip. Serve with celery sticks and cauliflower, if preferred.

Nutritional Info:

Calories 203 kcal, **Carbs** 13g, **Protein** 8g, **Fat** 13g

7. AIR FRYER PIZZA

Ingredients	
Pizza dough 1 dough of 12-inch, it will create 2 small pizzas	
22g	of Buffalo mozzarella
15ml	Olive oil
Optional toppings: parmesan cheese, fresh basil, pepper flakes	
225g	Tomato sauce

Instructions

1. The air fryer should be heated to 190° C. Spray oil into the air fryer basket. With paper towels, dry off the mozzarella.
2. **Cooking the Crust**: Stretch the pizza dough to fit the air fryer basket's size. Place it in the air fryer, then give it a small drizzle of about a teaspoon of olive oil. Cook for three minutes.
3. **Assemble:** Spoon a thin layer of tomato sauce over the precooked crust and add the buffalo mozzarella bits on top.
4. **Bake:** For approx. 7 minutes until the cheese is melted and the crust should be crispy. Just before serving, you may optionally add grated parmesan, basil, and pepper flakes.

Nutritional Info:

Calories 203 kcal, **Carbs** 52.6g, **Protein** 8g, **Fat** 12.6g

8. AIR FRYER SWEET POTATO FRIES

Ingredients	
0.5g	of paprika
0.4g	of garlic powder
10ml	of olive oil
2 peeled, medium sweet potatoes peeled	
0.3g	of black pepper
3g	of salt

Instructions

1. Set the air fryer's temperature to 193°C. Sweet potatoes should be peeled before being cut into uniform sticks 1/4 inch thick.
2. In a large bowl, mix the sweet potatoes with olive oil, garlic powder, salt, black pepper& paprika.
3. Depending on the basket size, cook them in 2 or 3 batches, without packing the basket too tightly, until they are crispy. 12 minutes, with a halfway turn, is what I advise. Depending on your air fryer, this might differ.
4. Immediately serve with your preferred dipping sauce.

Nutritional Info:

Calories 149 kcal, **Carbs** 27g,

Protein 2g, **Fat** 4g

9. AIR FRYER CHICKEN SAUSAGE

Ingredients

4 precooked chicken sausages, 85g each

Instructions

1. For five minutes, preheat the air fryer to 190° C.
2. Put as many air fryer sausages as the appliance can accommodate.
3. The chicken sausage should be air fried for 8 to 10 minutes, turning them over halfway through. 74 degrees Celsius should be the interior temperature.
4. Models of air fryers may differ, and some fry at higher temperatures than others. If, by chance, your model cooks quickly the first time you prepare the dish, keep a careful check on the sausage cooking time. Adjust the cooking time as necessary to heat them thoroughly and brown them to your preference.

Nutritional Info:

Calories 170 kcal, **Carbs** 4.6g, **Protein** 13g, **Fat** 11g

10. AIR FRYER MINI CHIMICHANGAS

Ingredients	
1 chopped onion	
245g	of sour cream
354g	of shredded Monterey Jack cheese
45g	of ground beef
1 envelope of taco seasoning	
177ml	of water
14	eggs roll wrappers
1 can (59g) of drained and chopped green chiles	
1 lightly beaten, large egg white	
Salsa	
Cooking spray	

Instructions

1. Beef and onion should be fried over medium heat in a large pan. Empty it. To a pot of boiling water, add the taco seasoning and swirl to combine. Reduce heat to low and simmer, stirring occasionally for 5 minutes. Take it off the burner and let it cool down for a while.
2. Set the air fryer to 190° C. Mix the cheese, sour cream, and chilies in a large bowl. Add beef mixture and stir. Place an egg roll wrapper in the work area so that the corner faces you. Put 43g of the filling in the middle. Fold the sides in and fold the bottom third of the wrapper over the filling.
3. Apply egg white to the top tip; wrap up to seal. Use the leftover wrappers and filling to repeat. (Keep the leftover egg roll wrappers wrapped with waxed paper to prevent them from drying out.)

4. Place the chimichangas on the oil sprayed tray in the air fryer basket in one even layer and oil spray them as well. Cook for 3 to 4 minutes on each side or until they turn golden brown. Serve hot with salsa and more sour cream on the side.

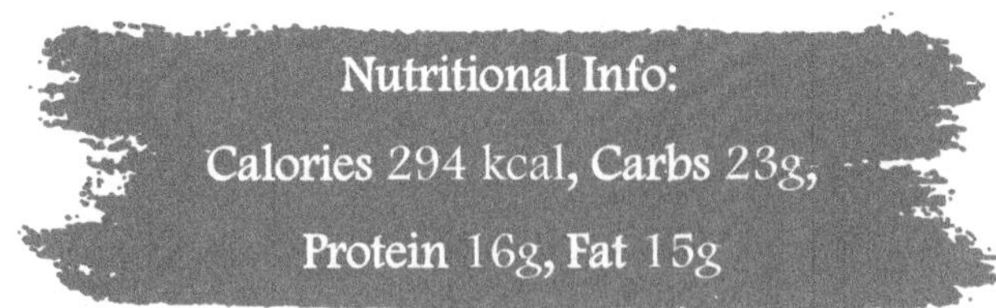

Nutritional Info:

Calories 294 kcal, **Carbs** 23g, **Protein** 16g, **Fat** 15g

11. AIR FRYER ANTIPASTO EGG ROLLS

Ingredients	
12	slices of provolone
12	egg roll wrappers
225g	of shredded mozzarella
36	slices of pepperoni
12	slices of deli ham
127g	of sliced pepperoncini
25g	of grated Parmesan
15ml	Vegetable oil if needed

Instructions

1. On a spotless surface, arrange an egg roll wrapper as a diamond with provolone slice in the middle. Add 1 slice of ham, three slices of pepperoni, and a generous amount of pepperoncini & mozzarella on the top. Wrap the sides and bottom firmly in. Roll gently, then, seal the fold with a few water drops.
2. Air fry the egg rolls in batches for 12 minutes at 200° C, turning halfway through, until browned.

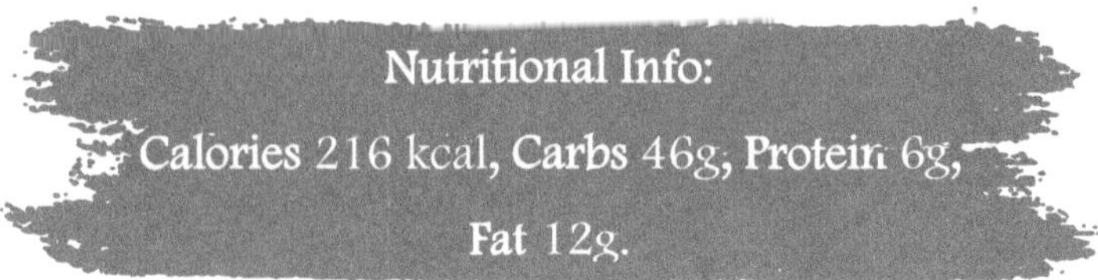

12. AIR FRYER CAULIFLOWER TOTS

Ingredients
Nonstick cooking spray
1 pack of (454g.) frozen cauliflower tots

Instructions

1. Set the air fryer to 200 degrees C. Spray some oil cooking spray on the air fryer basket.
2. Air fry the cauliflower tots in batches if required, adding as many as possible to the basket while ensuring they do not touch.
3. Air fry for 6 minutes in the heated air fryer. Tots should continue to cook for an additional 3 minutes after being turned over and heated through, and serve.

Nutritional Info:

Calories 147 kcal, **Carbs** 20g, **Protein** 2.7g, **Fat** 6.1g

13. AIR FRIED BAKED CHICKEN BREASTS

Ingredients	
10ml	of Olive Oil
1-4	skinless Chicken Breast
1.5g	of table salt (for each piece of chicken)
0.4g	of Garlic Powder (for each piece of chicken)
0.5g	of black Pepper (for each piece of chicken)

Nutritional Info:

Calories 203 kcal, **Carbs** 15g,

Protein 20g, **Fat** 4.5g

Instructions

1. Drizzle olive oil over the chicken breast & coat it well.
2. Sprinkle pepper, salt, and garlic powder on one side & Season the other side next.
3. Place the seasoned chicken in the preheated air fryer.
4. Air fry for 9 minutes at 182° C. After that, flip the chicken breast over and air fry it for 9 minutes. Smaller chicken breasts take less time to cook than larger ones do.
5. Immediately open the air fryer to prevent it from continuing to cook in the heat.
6. Use a meat thermometer to measure the doneness in the thickest area. 70°–71° C should be the temperature. If it is less, close the air fryer's cover and let the chicken breast cook for a few minutes in the same heat. Check it again.
7. Set it on a platter, cover it with foil loosely, and let it rest for 5 minutes. It will keep cooking in the lingering heat, then measure the temperature in 5 minutes. A minimum of 74 degrees Celsius should be maintained.
8. You may serve right away or preserve the leftovers for another dish or meal prep.

CHAPTER NO: 4

Air Fryer Dinner Recipes

Putting a meal on the table has never been simpler, thanks to these simple air fryer dinner ideas! After a hectic day, these are the ideal fast and simple meals to offer. You won't work up a sweat while making these air fryer supper dishes, which are very adaptable. Why work in the kitchen for hours when the air fryer can do it all? This list includes foods for every taste, from traditional dishes to contemporary cuisine. The days of worrying about what to serve for dinner are behind you, and your new favorite dishes are here.

1. HOMEMADE CANNOLI

Ingredients	
12.5g	Granulated Sugar
15g	All-Purpose Flour
227g	of Butter
125ml	of Dry White Wine
Sea Salt to taste	
1 Egg Yolk	

Instructions

1. Powdered sugar, Ricotta, and ground cinnamon should be combined in a sizable bowl; set aside.
2. With a hand mixer, whip the whipping cream in a big bowl for about two minutes or until stiff peaks form. Before assembling your cannoli, stir the whipped cream into the ricotta mixture and keep it in the fridge.
3. If your air fryer needs to be heated up, do so at 200 degrees Celsius on the air fryer setting. Cut the dough into fourths, then place one of the fourths on a lightly dusted, completely clean work surface. Restock the refrigerator with the leftover dough.
4. The dough should be rolled out about 1/8 inch of thickness. Cut out 4-inch circles with a cookie cutter; you can get 4-5 circles, depending on how thin you rolled out the dough.
5. Cooking sprays the cannoli molds, wraps the dough over them, and uses a little water to seal the edges where they meet. Simply submerge your fingers in the water. To seal, gently press down. Repeat with the remaining dough circles you are handling.
6. Spray the air fryer basket's interior. Spray the dough's exterior. Golden browning takes 4 to 6 minutes in the air fryer. Take the shells off the cannoli forms by removing them with tongs. Be careful because they are very hot.
7. In a medium bowl, mix the flour, salt & sugar. Place aside. With a pastry cutter, incorporate the chilled butter &create coarse crumbs. For this, you may either use two butter knives, a fork, or your hands. Once mixed, add the egg yolk and wine; the mixture should be crumbly.
8. Press or knead the dough into a ball on a lightly floured, clean surface. Cover the filling with plastic wrap and refrigerate it while you prepare the rest of the ingredients.

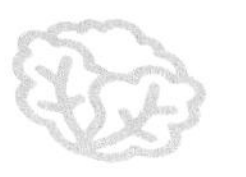

9. Continue by using the remaining shells. Allow the cannoli molds to cool completely in between batches if you plan to reuse them. Allow the shells to complete cooling. Pipe the stuffing into the shells once it has cooled. Dip the ends in pistachios or chocolate chips. Sprinkle with icing sugar before serving.

10. Keep in the refrigerator in an airtight container. Instead of arranging them and having them set, pipe the cannoli as you serve them if you can. The shells will stay crisp because of this.

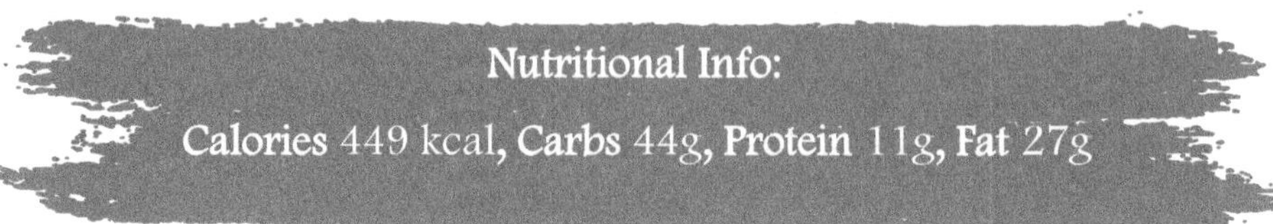

2. AIR FRYER BROWNIES

Ingredients	
45g	of unsweetened cocoa powder
2.5ml	of vanilla extract
62.5g	of all-purpose flour
150g	of sugar
57g	of unsalted butter melted
2	large eggs
15ml	of vegetable oil
1.5g	of salt
1.3g	of baking powder

Instructions

1. Oil spray a 7-inch baking pan generously or butter it to prepare it. Place it aside.
2. While you mix your brownie batter, preheat the air fryer by adjusting the setting to 165 degree Celsius and letting it run for approximately 5 minutes.
3. Add the all-purpose flour, butter, sugar, eggs, vanilla extract, baking powder, vegetable oil, & salt in a large bowl. Stir to blend completely.
4. It should be added and the top smoothed out in the baking pan.
5. In a preheated Air Fryer, bake for 15 minutes, or until a toothpick inserted in the center comes out largely clean.
6. Before removing and cutting, let it cool.

Nutritional Info:

Calories 385 kcal, **Carbs** 54g, **Protein** 6g, **Fat** 18g

3. AIR FRYER CHICKEN TAQUITOS

Ingredients	
225g	of softened cream cheese
420g	of shredded cooked chicken
2 minced chipotle peppers in adobo sauce	
1,5g	of cumin
1g	of chili powder
15ml	cooking spray
225g	of shredded Mexican cheese
12	small corn tortillas
Chopped fresh cilantro, Pico de gallo, and crumbled queso fresco for serving	

Instructions

1. Make the avocado sauce first. In a food processor, process avocado, lime juice, cilantro, & sour cream until smooth.
2. Add salt and pepper to taste. Mix well & keep it in the fridge, until ready to serve.
3. Note: You may use a blender or mash the ingredients by hand until smooth if you do not have a food processor.
4. Stir the chicken, chipotle peppers, cream cheese, cumin, chili powder, and chili sauce in a medium bowl until well combined.
5. Cover with a wet tea towel and microwave for half a minute to make tortillas more malleable.
6. Spread roughly 50g of filling towards one of the tortilla after adding a couple of teaspoons of cheese. Wrap firmly. Proceed with 5 more.
7. Oil the air fryer basket sparingly. Spray the tops with oil before adding the six taquitos, seam side down.

8. Served topped with queso fresco, avocado sauce, pico de gallo & cilantro.
9. For 6 to 7 minutes, air fry at 200° C.
10. For a second batch, repeat the process with the remaining tortillas.

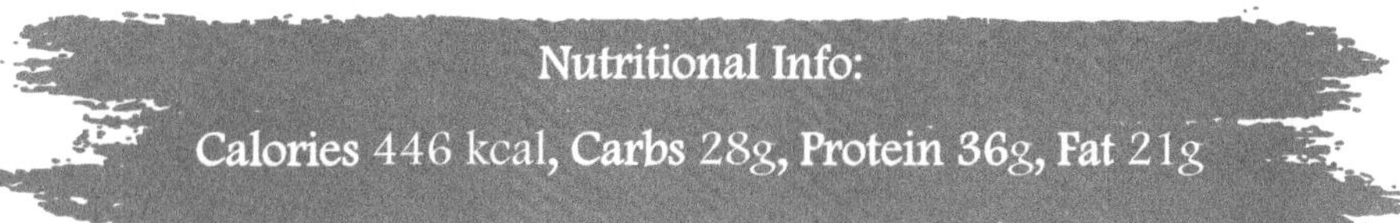

Nutritional Info:

Calories 446 kcal, **Carbs** 28g, **Protein** 36g, **Fat** 21g

4. AIR FRYER STEAK

Ingredients	
1g	Of freshly chopped rosemary
2	minced cloves of garlic
57g	of softened butter
1g	of freshly chopped thyme
1g	of freshly chopped chives
Kosher salt to taste	
1	bone-in ribeye of 590g.
Black pepper to taste	
2.5g	of freshly chopped parsley

Instructions

1. Mix butter & herbs in a small dish. Roll into a log in the middle of a piece of plastic wrap. Refrigerate for about 20 minutes to allow the ends to the firm after tightly twisting them together.
2. Use salt and pepper to season the steak generously.
3. Air fried the steak at 200 degrees for 12–14 minutes, flipping halfway through cooking time depending on the thickness of the meat.
4. Place small patof herb butter on steak before serving.

Nutritional Info:

Calories 301 kcal, **Carbs** 0.0g, **Protein** 23g, **Fat** 23g.

5. BRUSSELS SPROUTS CHIPS

Ingredients	
28g	of garlic powder
15ml	of oil
226g	of Brussels Sprouts
Pinch of salt to taste	
Black Pepper to taste	

Instructions

1. The Brussels sprouts should be put in a big dish. Then, after mixing everything well, add the oil. Mix the salt, garlic powder & black pepper, and stir once more to properly distribute the ingredients.
2. In your air fryer, arrange a few of the Brussels sprout leaves in one even layer. Work in batches is necessary since they probably won't all fit. Cook until crispy for 4 to 7 minutes at 190°C. Add the leftover Brussels sprouts to the dish. Remember that the first batch will take the longest (7 minutes), but subsequent batches will cook more quickly since the pan will already be heating (4-5 minutes).
3. Some Brussels sprout leaves will cook more quickly than others since they come in a variety of sizes. Check the Brussels sprouts around 1-2 minutes before the timer to avoid burning them.
4. Cut the bottom of the Brussels sprouts off by approximately 1/2 inch, and then take off any broken outer leaves. Peel the leaves off each sprout, starting at the base and working your way up to the center using your fingers. If the leaves do not fall off the stem, you may need to chop the Brussels sprouts a second or third time Continue doing so until you run out of leaves. For every sprout, repeat.

5. Remove any leaves that have already begun to crisp up before adding the remaining leaves back in to complete frying.
6. It is better to eat these Brussels sprout chips right away.

Nutritional Info:

Calories 74 kcal, **Carbs** 7.2g, **Protein** 2.6g, **Fat** 4.9g

6. AIR FRYER PORK CHOPS

Ingredients	
30ml	of extra-virgin olive oil
4 boneless (about one-inch thick) pork chops	
1.6g	of garlic powder
5.6g	of kosher salt
2g	of smoked paprika
2g	of onion powder
45g	of finely grated Parmesan
1g	of black pepper

Instructions

1. Use paper towels to dry the pork chops before applying oil to both sides.
2. Combine Parmesan, paprika, salt, onion powder, black pepper, garlic powder, in a medium bowl. Apply the Parmesan mixture evenly to the both sides of the pork chops, pressing it in place.
3. Place the chopsin one even layer in an air fryer basket. Air fry at 375° C for 9 minutes, turning once, or until a meat thermometer put in into the thickest portion of the pork chop reads 63° C.
4. Before serving, let the pork chop for approximately 10 minutes to rest.

Nutritional Info:

Calories 393 kcal, **Carbs** 3g, **Protein** 34g, **Fat** 26g

7. AIR FRYER CHICKEN TENDERS

Ingredients	
2	beaten large eggs
12	chicken tenders (566g)
50g	of seasoned breadcrumbs
Black pepper, to taste	
5.6g	of kosher salt
60g	of seasoned panko
lemon wedges for serving	
olive oil spray	

Instructions

1. Use salt and pepper to season the chicken.
2. The eggs should be put in a small bowl. The panko & breadcrumbs should be combined in a second bowl.
3. Shake off excess breadcrumb mixture after dipping chicken in egg, then place on a large plate or cutting board. Spray the chicken with oil on both sides.
4. Turn the air fryer on to 200° C.
5. Air fry the chicken in batches for 5-6 minutes on one side until it is cooked through and has a crunchy, light brown exterior.
6. Serve hot & enjoy.

Nutritional Info:

Calories 291 kcal, **Carbs** 16.5g, **Protein** 38.5g, **Fat** 7g

8. MOZZARELLA STICKS

Ingredients	
1g	of Italian seasoning
2.6g	kosher salt of salt
8 whole milk or low-fat mozzarella sticks	
1	large egg
60g	cup of panko breadcrumbs

Instructions

1. A mozzarella stick should be well coated after being dipped into the beaten egg. The stick should be well coated after being dipped into the dish of breadcrumbs.
2. Line them up so they are not touching a baking sheet with a rim lined with wax paper. Frost for no less than half an hour or up to an hour.
3. Take the mozzarella sticks out of the freezer, coat in whisked egg, next in the breadcrumb mixture, and return them to the freezer for 30-60 minutes.
4. Your air fryer should be at 200°C. Apply nonstick frying spray on the mozzarella sticks and the air fryer basket. When the outside is golden and crispy, air-fried the mozzarella sticks for 6 to 8 minutes (in batches if preferred or required, as space allowed).
5. Take out of the frying, let cool just long enough to prevent tongue burn, and then enjoy immediately!
6. Lightly beat the egg in a large, shallow basin.
7. Wax paper should be used to line a baking pan.
8. Mix the salt, breadcrumbs, and Italian seasoning in a second large, shallow basin.

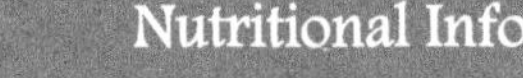

Nutritional Info:

Calories 163 kcal, **Carbs** 18g, **Protein** 7g, **Fat** 7g

9. AIR FRYER SALMON

Ingredients	
15ml	of olive oil
200g	of 4 salmon fillets
2g	of garlic powder
1g	of paprika
Tartar sauce for serving	
Lemon wedges for serving	
Salt and pepper to taste	

Instructions

1. Set the air fryer to 200° C.
2. Olive oil is applied to each fillet before being seasoned with salt, pepper, garlic powder & paprika. Depending on the thickness of the salmon, place it in the air fryer and cook for 7-9 minutes. Please be aware that air fryer times might vary.
3. With the basket open, use a fork to verify the food's doneness. If further time is needed, you may return the salmon for another one or two minutes.

Nutritional Info:

Calories 276 kcal, **Carbs** 1g, **Protein** 34g, **Fat** 14g

10. AIR FRYER ROTISSERIE CHICKEN

Ingredients	
2.5g	of paprika powder
2g	of onion powder
1g	of ground black pepper
1g	of garlic powder
15g	of sea salt
1g	of ground thyme
1g	of cayenne pepper
1 giblet removed from whole fryer chicken	
1g	of ground white pepper

Instructions

1. Let the air fryer preheat to 176° C.
2. Add the following ingredients to a bowl: paprika, salt, onion powder, black pepper, white pepper, cayenne, garlic powder& thyme.
3. Rub half the oil and half the spice mixture over the chicken.
4. Air fry for half an hour in the preheated air fryer. Take the chicken out of the pan with care.
5. Flip the chicken over. Dusting the leftover spice mixture on the other side after oiling it. Return to the air fryer and air fry for 30 minutes until the meat is cooked at the bone and the juices remain clear. 74 degrees C should be shown on an instant-read thermometer injected into the densest section of the thigh, close to the.

44ml	of vegetable oil

6. Remove from the fryer, wrap in two sheets of aluminum foil & set aside for 10 minutes to rest before slicing.

Nutritional Info:

Calories 351 kcal, **Carbs** 1.5g, **Protein** 42.8g, **Fat** 18.3g.

11. BUTTERMILK FRIED CHICKEN

Ingredients	
473ml	of buttermilk
700g	of chicken thighs, skinless &boneless
60g	of panko bread crumbs
120g	of all-purpose flour
3g	of ground black pepper
15g	of seasoned salt
15ml	cooking spray

Nutritional Info:

Calories 335 kcal, **Carbs** 33.2g, **Protein** 24.5g, **Fat** 12.8g

Instructions

1. Chicken thighs should be put in a shallow casserole dish. Chicken should be covered with buttermilk and chilled for four hours or overnight.
2. Achieve a 190 degrees C air fryer temperature.
3. Mix flour, seasoning salt, and pepper in a gallon-sized resealable plastic bag. Put chicken thighs in seasoned flour and dredge. Buttermilk should be reapplied after coating with panko bread crumbs.
4. Spray some cooking oil on the air fryer basket. Make sure none of the chicken thighs are touching when you arrange half of them in the basket. Each chicken thigh's top should be sprayed with cooking spray.
5. Prepare in a warm air fryer for 15 minutes. After you've flipped the thighs, spray the chicken's upper parts with oil again. Ten minutes, or until a knife inserted into the thickest part of the bird comes out clean.
6. In the middle, a meat thermometer inserted should register at least 74 degrees. Repeat with the remaining chicken.

12. BRUSSELS SPROUTS

Ingredients	
15ml	Olive Oil
Brussels Sprouts	
Garlic for garnishing	
Salt and Pepper to taste	

Instructions

1. Cut the Brussels sprouts in half after trimming.
2. If you want the sprouts to be softer in the middle, immerse them in water for 10 minutes.
3. Dry off and drain the sprouts. Add them to the air fryer after tossing them with oil and seasonings.
4. Cook for 5 minutes at 190 degrees C before tossing. After 5 more minutes of cooking, stir once more. Air fry for 2 to 4 minutes after mixing the garlic (if using).
5. Enjoy after adding any preferred toppings!

Nutritional Info:

Calories 216 kcal, **Carbs** 49.6g, **Protein** 7g, **Fat** 12g

13. AIR FRYER PINEAPPLE CHICKEN

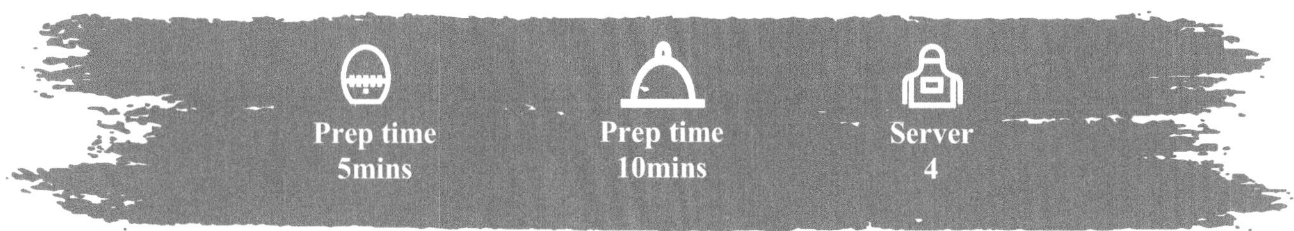

Ingredients For the Grilled Chicken	
14g	of butter
2 raw chicken breasts	
0.3g	of pepper
1g	of salt
For the Pineapple sauce	
10ml	of water
½ cup	of pineapple juice

Instructions

1. Set the air fryer to 193°C.
2. Stir salt and pepper into the melted butter and add it to the casserole. Coat chicken breasts on both sides before air frying them for 10–15 minutes. flipping halfway through. When the inside reaches 165 degrees, they are done. Give the chicken at least five minutes to rest.
3. Then, prepare the pineapple sauce by combining the brown sugar, pineapple juice, soy sauce, chopped ginger& garlic in a small pot and simmering for five minutes.
4. In another dish, combine the cornstarch and water; mix the mixture into the sauce. Turn the heat off after one more minute of tossing and simmering.

1 color	of minced garlic, 3g
56g	of low-sodium soy sauce
1/4 cup	of brown sugar
0.7g	of ground ginger
5g	of cornstarch
Optional	
chunks of canned or fresh pineapple (juice drained)	

5. Cut the resting grilled chicken breasts into long strips, then, either completely cover the chicken with sauce or spoon sauce on top before serving.
6. If preferred, add pineapple pieces, either fresh or canned.

Nutritional Info:

Calories 503 kcal, **Carbs** 15g, **Protein** 46g; **Fat** 5g

CHAPTER NO: 5

Air Fryer Desserts and Snacks

You can create everything from fried Oreos to Corn Dogs and even churros! Whether you want sweets or snacks, these desserts and snacks in the air fryer are just what you need. I've put together a selection of desserts and snacks you may make in the air fryer to consume after lunch or as a special treat.

1. PEANUT BUTTER EXPLOSION CAKES

Without a doubt, these molten cakes are the greatest. They may be delicately cooked to absolute deliciousness in your Air Fryer. The cake is quite rich and has a deliciously creamy core.

Ingredients	
170g	of chocolate chips
113g	of butter, plus more for the ramekins
30g	of all-purpose flour
4ml	of pure vanilla extract
2	large eggs, plus two egg yolks
25g	of unsweetened cocoa powder
50g	of powdered sugar
2.5g	of kosher salt
237ml	of water
60g	of peanut butter

Instructions

1. 4 ramekins should be butter-greased. Melt chocolate chips& butter in a small bowl in microwave, with 30-second intervals until melted. Whisk in the vanilla, egg yolks, powdered sugar, and eggs until well whisked. Whisk in the flour, salt, and cocoa powder until just mixed.
2. Only halfway fill the ramekins with batter, and cover each with a heaping spoonful of peanut butter. Add the remaining batter on top. Wrap foil securely around the ramekins.
3. Air fry in batches, if required, put the ramekins in the air fryer basket. Remove foil and continue cooking for an additional 6 minutes after 12 minutes at 190° C.
4. Ramekins should be removed from the air fryer with care. Run a knife or offset spatula along the edges. Before serving, invert onto a dish and sprinkle with confectioner's sugar.

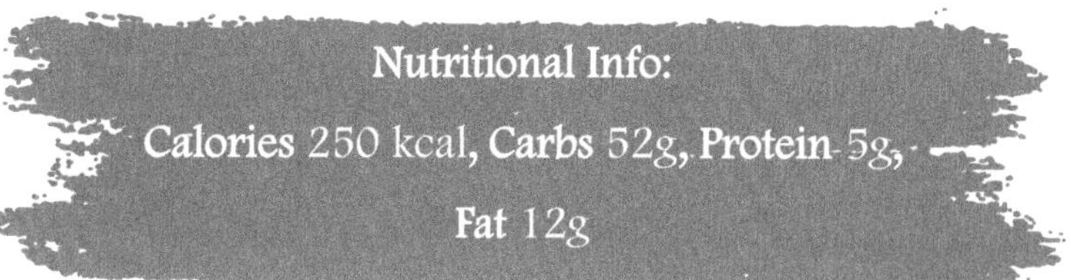

2. BLOOMIN' APPLES

Ingredients	
13g	of packed brown sugar
57g	of melted butter
Cooking spray	
2g	of ground cinnamon
12g	of granulated sugar
4	apples
8 chewy caramel squares	
Caramel for serving	
Vanilla ice cream for serving	

Instruction

1. Mix the sugars, cinnamon & butter in a small bowl.
2. Each apple's top should be cut off, and the core should be removed using a melon baller (or a teaspoon). Cut the apple into two circles with a paring knife. Slice crosswise through the apple, cut side down, careful not to cut into the core.
3. Two caramel pieces should be placed into each apple, followed by a butter mixture brushed on top. Put sliced apples in the air fryer's basket. Bake for fifteen to twenty minutes at 177° C.
4. Serve warm with ice cream and caramel sauce.

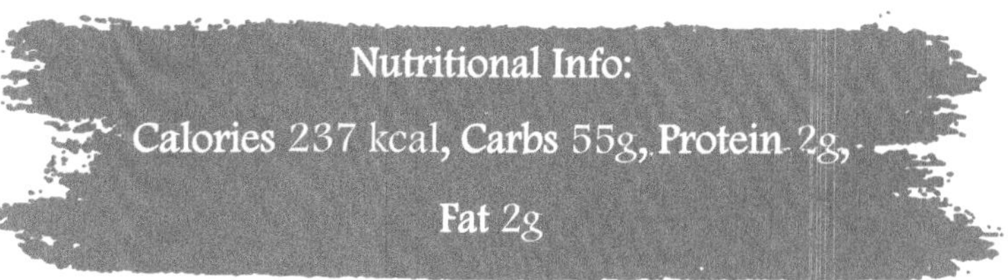

3. BANANA PANCAKE DIPPERS

Ingredients BANANA PANCAKE DIPPERS	
14g	of butter
3 bananas, sliced lengthwise	
Melted chocolate for dipping	
1 batch of prepared pancake batter	
PANCAKE BATTER	
14g	of baking powder
180g	of all-purpose flour

Ingredients

BANANA PANCAKE DIPPERS

1. Mix the flour, brown sugar, salt &baking powder in a bowl.
2. Mix the milk, sour cream, and eggs in a separate bowl before adding each egg one at a time. Stir in vanilla and mix.
3. Mix the dry ingredients with a spatula after adding the wet ones.

FOR THE AIR FRYER

1. Cooking spray should be used to oil the parchment paper of the air fryer basket.
2. Put bananas on parchment paper in one even layer after dipping them in pancake batter in batches.

5g	of kosher salt
26g	of brown sugar
177ml	of whole milk
2 large eggs	
5ml	of vanilla extract
123g	of sour cream

3. Cook for 15 minutes at 177° C until golden.
4. For dipping, serve with melted chocolate.

Nutritional Info:

Calories 105 kcal, **Carbs** 20g, **Protein** 2g, **Fat** 2g

4. CHURRO CHIPS

Ingredients	
14g	of melted butter
192g	of granulated sugar
6	medium flour tortillas
6g	of cinnamon

Instructions

1. Each tortilla is divided into 8 triangles. Make sure both sides of the tortillas are covered with butter before tossing them.
2. Add cinnamon & sugar in a medium bowl. Toss the tortillas in cinnamon-sugar while working in batches.
3. Put the tortillas in the basket in one even layer while working in batches. Air fry for 6 minutes at 190°.

Nutritional Info:

Calories 44 kcal, **Carbs** 8g, **Protein** 1g, **Fat** 1g.

5. APPLE CHIPS

Ingredients	
24g	of granulated sugar
2	thinly sliced apples
2g	of cinnamon

Instructions

1. Apples should be mixed with sugar and cinnamon in a big basin. Apples should be placed in one even layer in the air fryer basket as you work in batches (some overlap is okay).
2. Bake for about 12 minutes at 177° with flipping every 4min.

Nutritional Info:

Calories 98 kcal, **Carbs** 27g, **Protein** 0g, **Fat** 0g

6. LOW CARB CRUSTLESS CHEESECAKE

A cheesecake without a crust that is simple to make and has all the delicious taste you adore. So you may spend more time enjoying and less waiting, this food is swiftly made using a blender and an Air Fryer.

Ingredients	
2.5ml	of lemon juice
177ml	of zero-calorie sweetener
2	eggs
30g	of sour cream
454g	of cream cheese softened to room temperature

Instructions

1. Set the air fryer's temperature to 175° F.
2. Whisk the eggs & lemon juice until well combined. Blend in the cream cheese &sour cream until lump-free& well mixed. It will get creamier the more you whisk it.
3. Fill 2 4-inch spring form pans with batter, & air fry for 8-10 minutes or until firm.
4. Let the pan to cool fully. Keep in the fridge for at least 2-3 hours. Enjoy!

Nutritional Info:

Calories 250 kcal, **Carbs** 32g, **Protein** 5g, **Fat** 12g"

7. AIR FRYER FRIED OREOS

Ingredients	
1	crescent sheet roll
9	Oreo cookies

Instructions

1. Spread the pop crescent out on the table. Line up and cut 9 equal squares with a knife.
2. Grab nine cookies, then, wrap them in those squares.
3. Set the air fryer to 180° C of heat. Air fry wrapped cookies in one even layer for 4 minutes, stirring and flipping once.
4. If desired, garnish with cinnamon or powdered sugar.

Notes

- For the recipe, any flavor of Oreo cookie can be used. The best are probably double stuffed!
- Avoid overcooking cookies because they will dry out.
- Use any other preferred cookies with this recipe. Try out different shapes and colors, such as squares. Children would adore that!

Nutritional Info:

Calories 67 kcal, Carbs 10g, Protein 1g, Fat 3g

8. AIR FRYER SPINACH FETA TURNOVERS

Ingredients	
1 package (38g) of chopped spinach	
2 large eggs	
169g	of crumbled feta cheese
0.5g	of pepper
Refrigerated tzatziki sauce, optional	
2 minced garlic cloves	
1 tube of (13.8g)	of refrigerated pizza crust

Instructions

1. Set the air fryer to 218° C. Add egg to a bowl & whisk; one spoonful should be saved. Spinach, pepper, feta cheese, garlic, and the remaining beaten eggs should all be combined.
2. Roll the pizza dough into a 12-in. square into four 6-in. pieces. Squares. Add roughly 10g of the spinach mixture to each square. Triangle-shaped fold; squeeze corners together to seal. Slit the top and brush with the saved egg.
3. Triangles should be placed on an oil sprayed in the air fryer basket in one even layer, if possible, in batches. Air fry for 10 to 12 minutes, until they turn golden brown. Serve with tzatziki sauce, if preferred.

Nutritional Info:

Calories 361 kcal, **Carbs** 51g, **Protein** 17g, **Fat** 9g

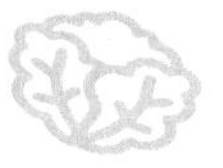

9. AIR FRYER CORN DOGS

Ingredients

1 package of frozen corn dogs

Nutritional Info:

Calories 210 kcal, **Carbs** 47g, **Protein** 7.5g, **Fat** 1g

Instruction

1. Your air fryer needs two minutes of 200° C heating.
2. Cooking spray should be applied lightly to the air fryer racks. The frozen corn dogs should be arranged in one even layer with at least 12 inches of space between each one because hot air is forced into the food in air fryers, so space enables the hot air to circulate. This means that while the corn dogs are air frying, you won't need to turn them over.
3. The corn dogs are air fried for eight minutes. Let them cool for approximately 2 minutes before serving.

10. AIR FRYER MUSHROOM ROLL-UPS

Ingredients	
226g	of large portobello mushrooms, finely chopped and gills discarded
112g	of whole-milk ricotta cheese
29g	of EV olive oil
1g	of dried oregano
1g	of dried thyme
1g	of salt
1g	of crushed red pepper flakes
1 pack of (227g) of softened cream cheese	

Instructions

1. Add oil to a pan & heat over medium flame. Add the mushrooms and cook for 4 minutes. Add salt, pepper flakes, thyme & oregano. Cook for 4-6 minutes or until mushrooms are browned. Let it cool.
2. Combine the cheeses, then, thoroughly fold in the mushrooms. Place 3 tablespoons of the mushroom mixture in the center of every tortilla's bottom. Roll firmly, then, use toothpicks to secure.
3. Heat the air fryer to 200° C. Place roll-ups in the air fryer basket in batches on an oil sprayed basket and spritz with cooking spray. Cook for 9 to 11 minutes or until they turn golden brown. Discard toothpicks after roll ups have cooled enough to handle. Serve with chutney.

Nutritional Info:

Calories 291 kcal, Carbs 31g, Protein 8g, Fat 16g

11. AIR FRYER CALAMARI

Ingredients	
2.5g	of salt
1 lightly beaten large egg	
60g	of all-purpose flour
125ml	of 2% milk
0.5g	teaspoon of pepper
60g	of panko bread crumbs
15ml	of Cooking oil
2.5g	of seasoned salt
224g	of cleaned frozen or fresh calamari (squid), thawed and sliced into 1/2-inch rings

Instructions

1. Put in a dish of frozen french fries and set the air fryer to 200 degrees. In a small bowl, whisk together the flour and salt. In a separate shallow dish, combine the egg and milk. In a third, smaller bowl, combine the bread crumbs, salt, and pepper.
2. To properly prepare calamari, first coat it in flour, then in an egg wash, and last in bread crumbs.
3. Calamari should be placed in single layers on an oil sprayed air fryer basket air fry in batches after being oil sprayed.
4. Air fry for 4 min. Spray with cooking spray after flipping. Air fry for 3-5 more minutes or until they turn golden brown.

Nutritional Info:

Calories 11 kcal, **Carbs** 1g, **Protein** 1g, **Fat** 0g

12. AIR FRYER QUINOA ARANCINI

Ingredients	
2 lightly beaten eggs, divided	
185g	of cooked quinoa
Or	
1 pack of (255g.) of quick cooking quinoa	
21g	of shredded Parmesan cheese
15ml	of olive oil
1g	of garlic powder
6g	of minced fresh basil

Instructions

1. Set the air fryer to 88° C. Cook the quinoa as per instructions on the box to prepare it. Add seasonings, 30g bread crumbs, egg, oil, basil& Parmesan cheese.
2. Cut into six pieces. Each serving should be formed into a round by fully encircling a cheese cube.
3. Distribute the last egg and half of the bread crumbs into two small dishes. Roll quinoa balls with bread crumbs after egg dip.
4. tray; mist with cooking spray. Cook for 6 to 8 minutes or until they turn golden brown. Serve with pasta sauce.

50g	of seasoned bread crumbs, divided
2.5g	of salt
0.5g	of pepper
6 cubes of mozzarella cheese	
Warmed pasta sauce, optional	
Cooking spray	

5. Place in air fryer basket on oiled tray; mist with cooking spray. Cook for 6 to 8 minutes or until they turn golden brown. Serve with pasta sauce.

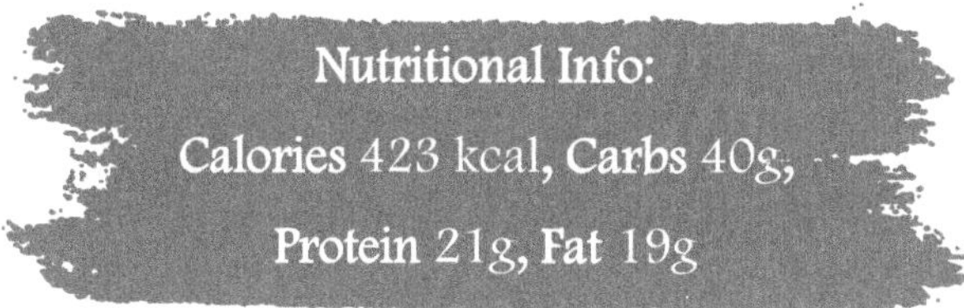

Nutritional Info:

Calories 423 kcal, **Carbs** 40g, **Protein** 21g, **Fat** 19g

13. AIR FRYER NASHVILLE HOT CHICKEN

Ingredients	
28g	of hot pepper sauce, divided
30ml	of dill pickle juice, divided
5g	of salt divided
120g	of all-purpose flour
30ml	of dill pickle juice, divided
1/2	of teaspoon pepper
2g	of paprika
Cooking spray	
117.5ml	of olive oil
118ml	of buttermilk
26g	of dark brown sugar

Instructions

1. Combine 14g hot sauce & 15ml of pickle juice, and half of the salt in a bowl or shallow dish. Chicken is added; marinate it well. Keep in the fridge for at least one hour. Drain the chicken, then discard the marinade.
2. Preheat the air fryer to 190 degrees Celsius. In a small bowl, combine the flour, pepper, and the remaining salt. Combine the buttermilk, egg, and 15ml of pickle juice, and 14g of the spicy sauce in a separate shallow basin. Shake off extra flour after coating the chicken on both sides. Before dipping again, coat with the egg mixture.
3. Cook the chicken, in one even layer on a tray that has been oil sprayed and placed in the air fryer basket. Cook for 5 to 6 minutes or until they turn golden brown. Flip & Spray with cooking oil. Cook for another 5 to 6 minutes or until they turn golden brown.

10.5g	of cayenne pepper
1 large egg	
2g	of chili powder
Dill pickle slices	
1g	of garlic powder

4. Add the rest of the ingredients to a bowl, whisked together, over the cooked chicken, and toss to coat.
5. Serve hot.

Nutritional Info:

Calories 203 kcal, **Carbs** 52.6g, **Protein** 8g, **Fat** 12.6g

14. AIR FRYER BEEFY SWISS BUNDLES

Ingredients	
454g	of ground beef
26g	of ground beef
17g	of Worcestershire sauce
3g	of minced garlic
113g	of shredded Swiss cheese
44g-88g	of sliced fresh mushrooms
2.5g	of salt
1.5g	of paprika
1 sheet of thawed frozen puff pastry	
0.8g	of crushed dried rosemary
0.5g	of pepper

Instructions

1. Prepare the air fryer for 190 degrees Celsius cooking. In a skillet over medium heat, brown the beef and add the onion and mushrooms; cook for 8 to 10 minutes, or until the meat is cooked through and the mushrooms are mushy. Tear up the steak you just cooked. Toss in the garlic and continue cooking for another minute. Drain. Put in the Worcestershire sauce and spices. Remove it from the burner and set it aside.
2. Puff pastry should be rolled out on a lightly floured board to a 15-by-13-inch rectangle. Generating four 7 1/2-by-6 1/2-inch rectangles is the next step. Place 17g of potatoes in the center of each square and spread to within 1 inch of the edges. On top of each serving, layer 21g and 255g meat mixture.

160g	of refrigerated mashed potatoes
30ml	of water
1 large egg	

3. Combine an egg wash with water and brush the pastry's edges. Bring the opposing pastry corners over each bundle and seal with a pinch. Use the remaining egg mixture to brush. In batches, arrange pastries one layer in the air-fryer basket; air fry until they turn golden brown, 10-12 minutes.

Nutritional Info:

Calories 706 kcal, **Carbs** 44g, **Protein** 35g, **Fat** 42g

15. AIR FRYER EGG ROLLS

Ingredients	
550g	of fresh bean sprouts
474ml	of hot water
454g	of ground chicken
6 chopped green onions	
3 garlic cloves, minced	
1 jar (311g)	of Chinese-style barbecue sauce
6g	of minced fresh ginger root
14g	of soy sauce or fish sauce
4.5g	of soy sauce

Instructions

1. Cover bean sprouts with boiling water in dish and let it rest for 5 minutes. Drain it.
2. In the meanwhile, boil the chicken in a large pot on medium flame for 6 to 9 minutes, or until it is cooked, then shred it. Add ginger, garlic, and green onions. Cook for another minute; drain. Transfer to a large bowl after stirring in 112g of the fish sauce, chinese-style sauce, and soy sauce. Clean the pot.
3. Cook and add the coleslaw mix, spinach, and drained bean sprouts in the same skillet for 4 to 5 minutes or until crisp-tender. Add to the chicken mixture by stirring. Cool a little.
4. Set the air fryer to 200° C. Place 43g of filling directly below the wrapper's center with the corner facing you on an egg roll wrapper. (Cover the leftover wrappers with a wet tea towel until ready to use.) Then, fold the lowest corner over the filling and wet the rest of the wrapper edges. Over the filling wrap the side corners toward the center. Egg rolls should be securely rolled, with the tip pressed to seal. Repeat.

1 package (38g) of chopped spinach	
1 package (395g) of coleslaw mix	
Cooking spray	
18	egg roll wrappers

5. In an oil sprayed air fryer basket, put the egg rolls in one even layer and spritz with cooking spray. Air fry for 8 to 12 minutes or until they turn golden brown. Turnover and give another spritz of cooking spray. Air fry for another 4-6 minutes or until they turn golden brown. Dish up with any leftover Chinese-style sauce.

Nutritional Info:

Calories 187 kcal, **Carbs** 33g, **Protein** 9g, **Fat** 3g

CONCLUSION

You have all the information you need to use your air fryer right now! Simply choose a recipe to get started quickly with your air fryer. Keep in mind that eating healthily doesn't need spending all your time in the kitchen or money on hand-delivered meals. All you have to do is try some new, delectable dishes that are likely to quickly become family favorites. The greatest thing you can do if you are one of those who cannot live without fried meals is to get an air fryer from the nearby shop. Instead of deep frying your favorite steak, fries, wings, vegetables, etc., you should air fry them. Compared to oil-frying, air-frying may considerably reduce the quantity of fat, calories, and other unhealthy substances in meals.

Your air fryer will rapidly surpass all other kitchen appliances in use! Air fryers drastically cut down on the amount of time you need to cook in the oven thanks to their quick pre-heat times. Similar to a small oven, an air fryer can handle practically everything you'd put in a regular oven or deep-fat fryer. Most brands and models have dishwasher-safe parts, are non-stick, and are simple to clean. Depending on the model, air fryers can bake, roast, and even dehydrate ingredients. They are no longer just for making chips. These appliances may be used as a rotisserie or a small oven in addition to convection cooking when you pick the air fryer option. This means you may cook meats and vegetables and roast meat using the same cooking tool. I recommend you try the dishes in this book and tell your coworkers and friends about what you discover. There is an advantage to purchasing a specialized air fryer; however, if air frying is all you intend to use it for. Your plate will have less fat; thus it makes air frying a better choice than deep frying.

IF YOU LIKE THIS BOOK, HELP ME BY LEAVING A REVIEW ON AMAZON!

Scan the QR code with your mobile phone and you can immediately leave a review,

or

1. Go to **Amazon** and click on "**My orders**"
2. Search for **this book** and click to go into details
3. Scroll down and click on Write a customer review

Share the pages you liked the most with and post them in the reviews.

Thanks a lot! See you soon.

Kerry Norris

Printed in Great Britain
by Amazon

33327503R00086